The Self-Coached Runner

Karen S. Perinchief

authorHOUSE®

AuthorHouse™
1663 Liberty Drive
Bloomington, IN 47403
www.authorhouse.com
Phone: 1 (800) 839-8640

Published by AuthorHouse 04/10/2018

ISBN: 978-1-5462-3588-0 (sc)
ISBN: 978-1-5462-3587-3 (hc)
ISBN: 978-1-5462-3586-6 (e)

Library of Congress Control Number: 2018903919

Print information available on the last page.

CONTENTS

Preface

Running can be easy and fun, even if you have asthma. Some people may say running is boring, while others find it enjoyable, but running is one of the most inexpensive ways to keep fit, lose weight, and stay in shape. There are no scheduled exercise classes, no waiting for machines at the gym, and no monthly fees. All you need is a pair of running sneakers, shorts, and a T-shirt.

As a Christian, I've included scriptures and other spiritual support in the book's text for encouragement. This book will help you to start running in an easy, simple way, even if you have asthma.

Acknowledgments

I give *all* the thanks and praise to our Father Jesus the Christ.
Many, many thanks to the following friends who encouraged me and gave me advice during training and races:

Edwina Arorash
George Jones
Hilton Brown
Jewell Eve
Donna Mae Arorash
Vernon Tankard
Leon James
Mark Albouy
Calvin Steede
Elvin Thomas
Mitchell Deshield
Clinton Curtis
The late Lugwick Cann
Karen Burchall
Mike Watson
Kevin Santucii
Margaret Burgess Howie
Cecil Whitecross

Beldwin Smith
Darnell Wynn
Lucy Lowe
Anthony Zuill
Beverley Hayward
Maybelline Black
Jerome Perinchief

Numerous other runners and walkers have assisted me during my training over the years. I want to say thank you all.

Introduction

Because I'm an asthmatic, I couldn't always do the training that my running buddies did. Well, I did it, but it caused me to be out of breath. The "healthy runners," as I called them, would run longer and faster than I could because my lungs could not take in enough air. Sometimes I thought maybe I needed to train harder, to spend more time training on the road or beach.

I felt out of place and sometimes embarrassed, constantly wheezing and coughing while running. I didn't want anyone to see me using my Ventolin inhaler. I would ask myself, *Why am I out here running if I can't breathe, if I'm out of breath, if I can't keep up, and if I'm feeling tired? Why am I having asthma attacks during training? Should I stop running and find another type of exercise, or should I continue running and find out what I need to do or what would work for me?* Still, I wanted to run because it was the least expensive exercise. Plus, I wanted to lose weight and stay fit and healthy. So I stopped training with my running group and started training on my own. I didn't know that asthma can be brought on while exercising. I knew that dust and certain sprays and perfumes made me cough but not exercise. Even when the weather was cold or humid, I had trouble breathing, so I had to use my Ventolin inhaler before and after my training runs—and sometimes during.

My doctor praised me for choosing running as an exercise, so I started to do some research to find out how I could control my breathing. I didn't know I needed to breathe through my nose more often to help prevent wheezing and coughing. I learned that my lungs needed to stay warm in order to breathe. Breathing (inhaling) through my nose would keep my lungs warm and help me breathe without wheezing and coughing.

I enjoyed training on my own at different times of the day—early morning runs, lunchtime runs, and evening runs. While training on my own, I used my inhaler when I coughed and wheezed, and I didn't feel out of place or embarrassed, as I did in front of my running group. I just didn't want anyone to know I had asthma. I wasn't aware of any other runners in our group who had asthma; I never saw anyone use an inhaler.

Chapter 1

Comparing a Christian to an Athlete

Over and over, the apostle Paul compares being a Christian to being an athlete. He speaks about running a race; he speaks about training and preparing for an event.

As Christians, we sometimes have doubts about our faith. As runners, we might have doubts about our ability to run a race. When you hear those voices of doubt within you, pick up the Bible, pick up your training journal, and remind yourself,

I can do all things through Christ, which strengthened me.
—Philippians 4:13

Suppose we train for a race like a Christian lives his or her life. The Christian will read the Bible and spiritually fast to hear from God more clearly. The Christian asks God for clarity of thought and for His guidance and help in order to focus attention and depend on God in every way. The Christian will meditate, asking God for wisdom and knowledge to memorize and reflect on a biblical passage. Then there's God's love, a gift that is offered to all. It's more than a feeling; it's a decision, it's an action, and it's a commandment by Jesus that we must love one another.

Then there is prayer. Prayer should come from your heart and communicate with God in your own words. Prayer is different for everyone—we pray on our knees, we bow our heads, we stand with our eyes open or closed. We write and read what God has told us to say.

Pray whichever way you feel comfortable.

Chapter 2

Pray Before You Run

Dear Father,

You gave me life; therefore,

I depend on you for everything—including the air I breathe.

Thank you for my health and my strength.

Watch over me as I run; keep my lungs filled with air and my legs strong.

Help me not to stumble and fall.

Father, I thank you for this day and every day as I finish my run.

In Jesus's name

Amen.

Chapter 3

Can We Run with Asthma?

Can we run with a chronic disease such as asthma? If we wish to run, then yes, we can run with asthma and have the assurance of God by asking Him for the ability to do it.

> And all things, whatever you shall ask in
> prayer, believing, you shall receive.
> Matthew 21:22

We can run if we prepare and apply ourselves, just like the apostle Paul, who spoke about the Christian being an athlete who commits to being fit by training and preparing for an event.

First, choose the event that you want to train for 26 mile marathon, half marathon, five miles or one mile., Decide when you will start your training, and set a date (for example, May 24).

Set your goal (for example, nine- to ten-minute mile, or complete the race in under two hours).

Set the distance (such as 26.2 miles).

Slowly start a combination of walking for five minutes and running at a comfortable pace for five minutes. Repeat this several times for a few weeks.

Then increase your walking time and running time.

You may do this three or four days a week. Your training doesn't have to be done consecutively. You may switch days to fit into your schedule.

Never compare yourself to other runners. Abstain from those negative things that might hinder your performance. Stop saying "I'm not a runner" or "I can't run."

Get out there, and just do it, like the young Greeks in the book of Timothy, who did physical training every morning:

Chapter 4

What Is Asthma?

Asthma is a chronic (or long-term) disease of the lungs, an inflammation that narrows the airways. Very little air gets to your lungs, making it difficult to breathe. Asthma causes repeated periods of wheezing, tightness of the chest, shortness of breath, and coughing.

Do your research and consult your doctor.

Prevent an attack and control your asthma.

Avoid using strong perfumes.

Avoid using air fresheners that are scented.

Avoid using scented laundry detergent.

Being overweight may contribute to asthma; therefore, try to maintain a healthy weight.

- Exercise.
- Reduce calorie intake.
- Watch how much you eat; chew and eat slowly.
- Stop eating when you are full. Do not stuff yourself.
- Pay attention to your symptoms, write them down, and consult your doctor.

Chapter 5

Should I Avoid Running if I Have Asthma?

Please consult your doctor before starting any form of strenuous exercise, especially if you have asthma.

With that caveat, no, you shouldn't avoid physical activity because of exercise-induced asthma. You can take steps to prevent asthma symptoms that allow you to maintain normal physical activity. In fact, many athletes—even Olympic athletes—are asthmatic, and they still compete. Many asthmatics have reached the pinnacle of their sports.

Record-breaking marathon runner Paula Radcliffe is one of Britain's best athletes, despite developing asthma when she was fourteen.

Jackie Joyner-Kersee, a track-and-field star who was a four-time Olympian and three-time Olympic gold medalist, was diagnosed with asthma while a freshman at UCLA. She hid her condition from her coaches and teammates.

Chapter 6

Monitor Your Asthma

Monitoring your asthma is especially important if you have exercise-induced asthma. To start running when you haven't done any sort of physical activity can be a shock to your body.

If you have exercise-induced asthma, you will experience tightness in your chest, coughing, and difficult breathing.

By keeping a journal, you can look back to see when you were most affected and what was going on weather-wise that may have contributed to your asthma. Write in your journal if you had difficulty breathing, for instance, or how many times you used your inhaler. Record the weather—was it hot, humid, or cold?

Some of my best runs have been in the rain. I guess that's because everything is being washed away, such as the pollen in the air and fumes from traffic, which are not great for asthmatics. Runners who have asthma should take a dose of their medicine, as directed by their physicians, a few minutes before a run to help control their symptoms. Using my inhaler has been helpful, especially in cold weather.

I always find the first one to three miles the most difficult. After that, my breathing is comfortable.

Be smart, and use your inhaler if you start wheezing, coughing, or having trouble breathing.

If you have a doctor's appointment, take your journal and show your physician what you recorded. That way your doctor can advise you, based on your information, whether or not you should continue running.

Be sure to carry your cell phone if you're running alone, or wear a Road ID, which you can purchase from a sports store. Write on your Road ID your name, contact number, and the information that you are asthmatic. In the event you need medical assistance, this can save valuable time for first responders and even save your life.

If you're running with a friend, tell him or her that you have asthma and explain what the signs are and where you keep your inhaler.

After a training run, a steamy shower might be beneficial, especially in the winter. It will help you relax and get your breathing back to normal. The steam from the hot water helps open the lungs.

Always carry your inhaler.

Chapter 7

Figure Out What Works for You

As a self-coached runner with asthma, you get to figure out what works for you.

All runners are not the same, and the assumption that they all need the same type of training is not true. We are individuals; each of us is unique. We are different because of our training needs, our body types, our blood types, our fitness levels, and our health. It's best to do a combination of training workouts:

- Endurance training—jogging, walking, cycling, swimming, dancing, and gardening; they all help keep your heart, lungs, and respiratory system healthy, as well as improve your overall fitness. Doing endurance training will make it easier to perform everyday activities.
- Flexibility training—helps the body stay limber. It gives you more movement to perform other exercises. Yoga is a good flexibility training.
- Strength training—builds muscle and makes them stronger.
- Balance training—helps prevent falls. Try the art of tai chi.

Training will come easily by putting one foot in front of the other and being consistent.

According to medical reports, people with asthma need to exercise. It helps strengthen your breathing muscles, as does having the correct medication prescribed by your physician.

If you are asthmatic or if you're not asthmatic but never have run or done any physical exercise, warming up before exercise is important. Walk first before you run.

Some of us may start out walking and then jog a little; that's okay. Some may start running ten to fifteen minutes at a time during their training, and that's okay as well. Different runners need different training schedules suited to their strengths, weaknesses, and fitness levels. Remember—we are all different.

Chapter 8

Benefits of Running and a Healthy Diet

You're starting this journey to train yourself to run with asthma. Runners run for different reasons. Some run for the enjoyment; others run because of the benefits gained from running. It's a good way to lose weight and get fit. Long runs and running several times a week—say, four or five times a week—will help you lose those extra pounds.

You'll also need to make smart food choices. It's been said you can eat whatever you want while exercising—that's not true, especially if you want to lose weight. Find out what food choices work for you.

I'm not a nutritionist, but I do know from experience that skipping a meal will not help you lose weight faster; it won't. You need energy to run, so don't skip meals or starve yourself. The "secret" is if you're eating fewer calories and spending more time running, you will lose weight.

Clear out processed foods that have no or few nutrients. Most processed foods contain high calories, salt, sugar, and fat, for taste. Canned or frozen foods are a better choice, but some also may contain high levels of salt, sugar, and fat. Also look for (and avoid) artificial flavorings.

Make a shopping list of healthy foods to keep in the house. I always have lemons, grapes, nuts, and apples in the house. These are my snack foods. Other healthy foods include yogurt, egg whites, blueberries, and oranges.

Runners must watch what they eat, so diet is important. If you have asthma, you may need to develop a new mind-set about food. Recognize which foods are good for you and which are not—and which trigger your asthma. Some foods will trigger an asthma attack and aggravate the symptoms. Some of these foods include cheese, cow's milk, peanuts, and some seafood.

The causes of asthma symptoms may vary from person to person.

Make a list of the specific foods that trigger your asthma, and plan to avoid those foods.

Chapter 9

Keep a Food Diary

Quick—what did you eat for lunch on Monday? I'll bet you have no idea, and that can be a problem if you are trying to lose or maintain your weight. Jot down every item of food and drink you consume during the day. After a week, look back and evaluate to see where you could fit in some fresh fruits and vegetables. The number of calories you should eat depends on your age, height, and gender, as well as your activity level.

Food Diary	Breakfast	Lunch	Dinner	Snacks	
Monday					
Tuesday					
Wednesday					

Thursday	Friday	Saturday	Sunday

Chapter 10

Find a Training Schedule

Your training plan should be reasonable and achievable. Look for a training schedule online, or ask a local running club to help you find your particular road-race schedule. Once you've done that, try to stick to the training schedule for that particular race. Find someone who you feel comfortable training with.

The race could be 5K (three miles), 10K (6.2 miles), half marathon (thirteen miles), or a marathon (twenty-six miles). Remember, you need to see what works best for you. It might be beneficial for you to run whichever race you choose as a training run first.

Once you've decided which race you're going to enter, and the race day approaches, sign up for the race, and pick up your race number. Sometimes you might get a race packet, which may include some great stuff, like a T-shirt, water bottle, energy bars, or discounts from sporting stores.

It's important to make sure you have enough energy while running, but never eat just before the race. Always eat one or two hours before the start of the race so that your body has time to digest your food.

Iron sharpens iron, and one man sharpens another.
Train together and encourage each other.
—Proverbs 27:17

Chapter 11

Running Shoes

Comfort is the key when purchasing a running sneaker. They are designed to absorb shock and to help your foot strike the ground properly. Please don't run in casual sneakers, which can lead to injury.

Each time you purchase a new pair of running sneakers, write the date in your journal, or mark it on your sneaker tongue; also keep a record in your journal of your miles run. As a general rule, you should be able to run five hundred miles on your new sneakers, but it depends on your body weight and the surface on which you run (e.g., road, beach, or trail). Worn-out running sneakers can lead to an injury.

When you purchase your sneaker buy a half size larger than you normally wear. This gives you more room for your toes to move forward with each stride.

In addition to number of miles run, some signs that your sneakers need replacing are shin splints or pain in your joints, especially around your knees.

Shoe brand is a personal choice. Select whichever brand name you prefer. Most sporting stores have salespeople who are knowledgeable about running shoes; they can help you with your selection. I always have worn Aces, which I find comfortable.

Having two pairs of sneakers is beneficial. You can alternate your sneakers if, for example, one pair gets wet, and wearing the other pair of sneakers will feel fresher than if you trained in the same ones every day.

As runners we tend to have a lot of sneakers. After training and running in them for several months, they wear down from pounding the trails and roads. Instead of throwing them away, donate them to a charity or thrift shop.

Chapter 12

Eating Prior to Running a Race

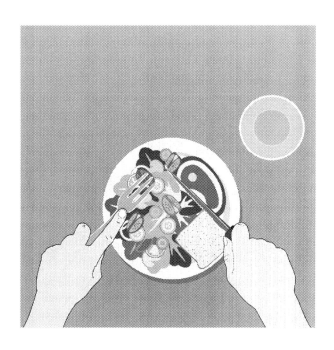

My favorite food to eat before a race is a toasted peanut butter-and-banana sandwich.

Another good option is a bowl of oat cereal with yogurt and honey or a smoothie.

Try not to eat fatty foods or fried foods because they will take a while to digest and will make you feel heavy, I choose the foods mentioned above because they are light, easy to digest, and won't make me feel full during my run.

Eat small meals throughout the day. This will help to give you energy and keep you from feeling hungry. Don't eat any foods unless you know how they'll affect you. Write down which foods work for you and which don't.

Other suggestions include the following:

- Trail mix
- Bananas
- Energy bars
- Apple slices
- Popcorn
- Nuts with raisins

We all have cravings, so please don't deny yourself the foods you crave and love.

Chapter 13

Celebrate Your Run

Celebrate if you get a runner's high, and you're breathing with ease.

For example, let your speed or your pace find you. Here's how: Start off slow and increase your pace. Your pace will slow back down, and then at some point in your slow run or jog, you will get a sudden increase in energy. Before you know it, you will start running relaxed and at a pace that feels comfortable. This doesn't happen all the time. When it does, enjoy it; it's a great feeling.

Don't beat yourself up if you can't get out and train due to weather or an appointment you may have. Feel proud of yourself. Take care of your body because it's the only one you have, and you can't replace it.

Tell yourself often that you're doing great with your training and reward yourself.

Stop driving yourself crazy; stop worrying, and stop putting pressure on yourself by comparing yourself to the other runners. Don't be discouraged if you couldn't do the training.

Focus on the positive. Remember that we make mistakes. We are human.

Take a few days off to rest after your training run. Your body needs rest to recover from training. Rest is necessary so that your muscles can repair, rebuild, and strengthen after training.

Do not be anxious about anything, but in everything,
by prayer and supplication, with thanksgiving, let
your requests be made known to God. And the peace
of God, which surpasses all understanding, will
guard your hearts and minds in Christ Jesus.
—Philippians 4:6–7

You're asking God to help you to avoid getting overly anxious during your training.

You're telling God what you need in order to stay committed to your training.

Chapter 14

Pick a Road Race

Pick the race in which you would like to compete—a race for a worthy cause, such as cancer research; or to raise money for a school trip to a foreign country. If you can't find any other reason to enter a race, sometimes running for a worthy cause can be a great way of staying motivated and can make your races more meaningful and fulfilling.

The race could be a local road race or a race that allows you to travel somewhere else in the world, such as Atlanta, New York, Washington, Puerto Rico, or Spain. Make the race fun. It could be included in a vacation you have planned.

Drive the race route several times, or look at the map and visualize where you would be at a certain point in the race. If you are able, run the course once to get a feel of the terrain.

Contact your local road-running clubs; they should know about a few upcoming races. You might consider becoming a member of a running club; that way you can be put on their mailing list.

You also can search the Internet. Talk to other runners; they could recommend a race for you and give you their views on the races and their overall experiences, which might help you to decide if that's a race you want to run.

Chapter 15

Keeping a Journal

I kept a journal when I first started running in 2003. I found that writing down my thoughts on how I was training was helpful for the next time I went out training. I also recorded the following:

- time of day and the date that I ran
- weather (e.g., too cold, too hot, just right, windy, light rain, very humid, a perfect day)
- how far I ran and how long it took me
- what I had eaten during that day
- how long my training runs were

I found this to be very helpful, as I took notes and compared the days, weeks, and months, even some years. Recording my mileage helped me to see the distances I had covered and to see my progress.

When I look back over the notes in my journal, I smile at how far I've come. I didn't give up. Sometimes I didn't want to be training, but once I got out and started to run, any negative feelings that I might have had just disappeared.

I was glad I kept a journal of my training. It kept me focused in reaching my goals. Keeping a journal of your training runs also can be beneficial in helping you decide whether you need to increase or decrease your miles, if you need to do speed work, or what time of the day you should stop eating before training. You might want to lose weight for a special occasion, or maybe you just want to train two or three days a week. Keeping a journal and having a goal means you have something to work forward to. Putting your goal on paper helps you to commit to doing the training. Writing it down is much more powerful than keeping it in your head; it will help you see how far you've come, what has worked for you, and what hasn't worked for you. You can note if you were frustrated, happy, or sad that day or if you were feeling strong, angry, or any other feelings that affected you. I found writing down my feeling helped with my emotional health.

Read your journal from time to time, and view it as a personal history of you. Be honest when writing down how you felt on your training day or where you may have eaten or craved a food and why. Use the self-knowledge in your journal to help refine your training.

You may experience variations in your training capabilities from day to day. Remember every runner is unique, and every training day is different. You may have days when your workout will be easy and it feels *great*. There also will be days when you're running and it feels like you just don't have the energy to do it, and you ask yourself, *Why am I doing this?* Do your best, and you will reach the finish line.

Chapter 16

Warming Up the Body

It's important to warm up the body before you start your run, as well as stretching. Start out walking for two or three minutes and then run for thirty seconds or two pole lengths. Do this for about twenty minutes to half hour. You know your body, and it may take longer than this for you to warm up; just remember to warm up slowly and adequately prior to training runs. More importantly, if you have asthma, breathe in through your nose instead of your mouth, especially in cold weather. Breathing in through your nose warms the air before it reaches your lungs.

In the summer, breathing can be a challenge because of the heat and humidity, as well as pollen and mold, which can affect your breathing. You will know your body has warmed up when you feel that slight sweat on your forehead, your breathing is easy, and you're not coughing or wheezing.

Chapter 17

Stretching

Stretching can help relieve pain in sore muscles after a run. Stretching increases your flexibility. Your muscles may be tense and tight, and stretching them could help improve your posture. Stretching may help improve your running performance as well.

While stretching your muscles, hold for a count of fifteen to thirty seconds without pain. Don't rush or hurry your stretch. Some runners stretch, and some don't. What works for one runner may not necessarily work for another. Stay relaxed, and don't tense you muscles. Breathe in and out slowly. Runners usually stretch the following parts of the body that are involved with running:

- Quadriceps (front of your thigh). While standing, pull your knee toward your bottom until you feel the stretch in your thigh.
- Hamstrings (back of the thigh). Bend forward at the waist with your hand in front toward the ground and your legs straight, not locking your knees. Try to touch your toes.
- Lower back. Lie on your back, and pull both knees to your chest. Put your hands behind your head. Slightly pull the head forward until the stretch is felt in the middle and lower back.

With a lunge stretch, or "runner stretch," both legs are together. Move one leg forward with your foot flat on the ground. Keep your weight even. Place both hands on your thigh and gently lean your body forward. You should feel the stretch in both legs. Hold each stretch for thirty seconds.

Before training, I encourage you to stretch, stretch, and stretch. I also love and appreciate a good stretch after a run. And I think it's important to stretch during your training runs. Perhaps you don't know the reasons why you should be stretching. It's a good idea to have a selection of stretches to show you the importance of stretching.

Various books and articles have different opinions on whether you should stretch before running or any exercise. For the beginner runner, run for five to ten minutes; then stop and stretch. This may vary, depending on how you're feeling on a given day.

I tend to stretch after my body is warmed up and I've run for about ten to fifteen minutes.

Stretching helps me with my flexibility, so I don't feel tight in certain parts of my body, like my legs, after a run.

Stretching after training will help you to avoid injuries. If you live near the ocean, do go into the sea after your training run and stretching as well. The water is refreshing. It may aid in relaxation and can help avoid injuries after a training run.

Our running club (Swans Running Club) always went in the water after a training run. It's been said that saltwater helps with recovery and/or injury, but some of those in our running club can attest that it reduced our muscle pain and soreness, as well as helped us to relax. If you're not near the ocean, I recommend using Epsom salts in a warm bath.

Chapter 18

Stay Hydrated— Drink, Drink

The most important advice I can give you is to drink eight to ten glasses of water a day, even if you're not training. You will know if you haven't drunk enough water during a training run because you will feel tired and won't be able to finish your training run. Always take your water bottle with you on your training run.

Water helps regulate your body temperature, so it's very important to drink more water on a hot day. Other beverages that help keep you hydrated are herbal teas, green tea, 100 percent fruit juices, and vegetable juices.

Remember that water is lost through urination, breathing, and sweating. We lose more water when we're active than when we're not active.

If you have pains in your joints and muscles, have a slight headache or constipation, or feel very thirsty, you may be dehydrated.

Do you not know that in a race all the runners run, but only one gets the prize? Run in such a way to get the prize.
—1 Corinthians 9:24

Even if the prize is personal, you entered a race and accomplished what you started.

You made it through to the finish line.

About the Author

Karen S. Perinchief has run in numerous races
and has not let her asthma slow her down.
She's not only a runner but has other social activities, and
loves the challenge of running and bowling in competitions
at home in Bermuda and overseas. Karen also does liturgical
dance and mime where she attends Mount Zion AME
Church. She is a Certified Health Coach, and has helped
motivate clients by listening, supporting and encouraging
them. She has a love for outdoors and vegetable gardening
is so satisfying to plant something in the earth and watch it
grow. I have grown cabbage, onions, broccoli, watermelon,
carrots, potatoes, red peppers, tomatoes, sweet basil and
fresh mint. Cooking is another one of my passions. I love to
experiment with different recipes by adding my own touch of
herbs and spices which becomes my own personal recipes.

Printed in the United States
By Bookmasters